For all the seedlings at Burgess Hill School – SG
With love to Chris, Chloe and Grace – SA

This edition published in Great Britain in 1998 and 1999 by
Macdonald Young Books, an imprint of Wayland publishers Ltd
61 Western Road
Hove
East Sussex
BN3 1JD

Find Macdonald Young Books on the internet at
http://www.myb.co.uk

Concept and design by Liz Black
Commissioning Editor Dereen Taylor
Language Consultant Ann Lazim, Centre for Language in Primary Education
Science Consultant Dr Carol Ballard

Text © Sam Godwin
Illustrations © Simone Abel
Book © Macdonald Young Books
M.Y.Bees artwork © Clare Mackie

A CIP catalogue record for this book
is available from the British Library

ISBN   07500 2497 6

Printed and bound in Asa, Portugal

A Seed in Need

A first look at the plant cycle

Sam Godwin

MACDONALD YOUNG BOOKS

A Seed in Need

A first look at the plant cycle

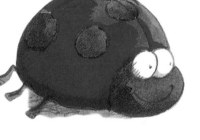

MACDONALD YOUNG BOOKS

Deep in the ground lies a seed.

7

8

That's right.

The sun warms the soil and the seed wakes up.

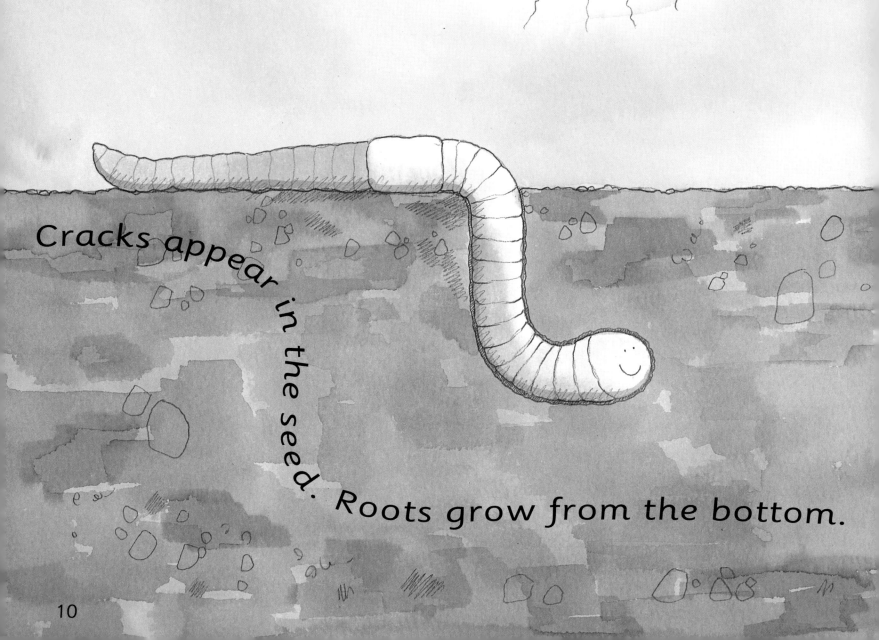

Cracks appear in the seed. Roots grow from the bottom.

11

The white shoot pushes its way through the soil.

12

The seedling turns greener. Its stem grows thicker

...and stronger and leaves appear on it.

Wow! Look how fast it's growing.

Children water the plant and give it plant food.

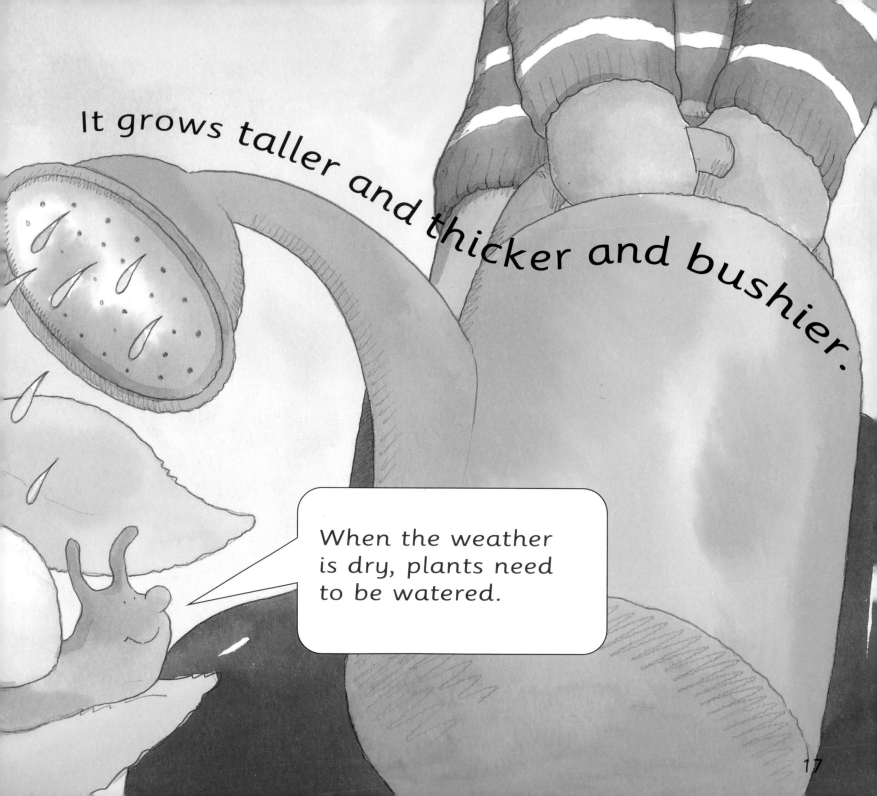

It's May and the garden is full of creatures

18

who shelter under the plant's leaves.

A bud appears on the plant. At first it is small

The bud turns into a beautiful flower.

Bees and butterflies come to visit it.

Look at the insects coming to drink nectar from the flower.

Summer is over and the flower begins to droop.

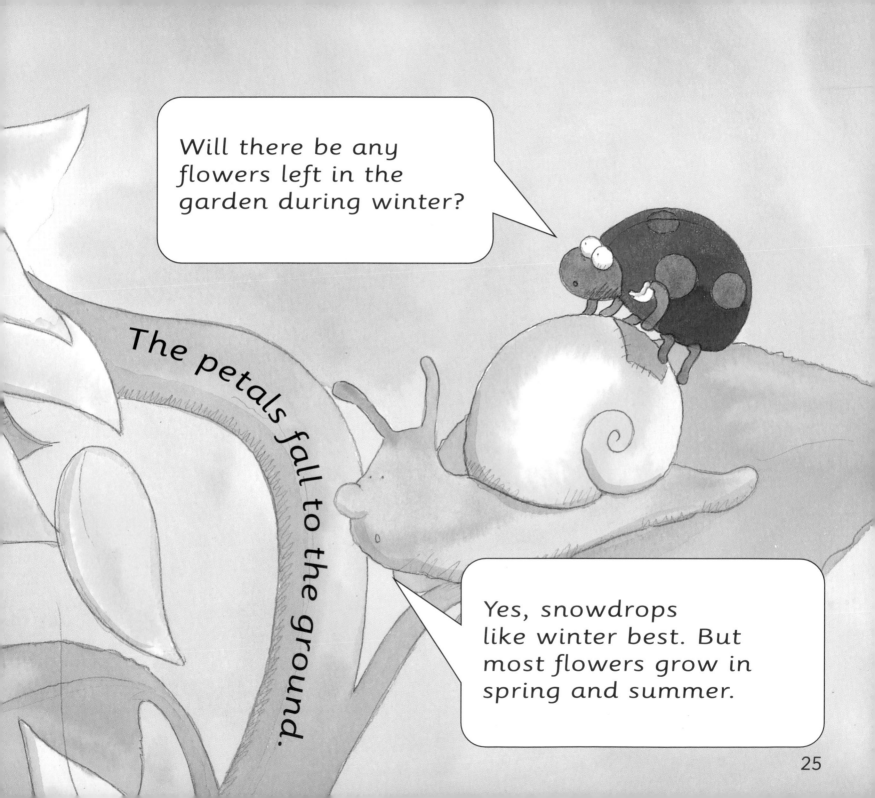

Will there be any flowers left in the garden during winter?

The petals fall to the ground.

Yes, snowdrops like winter best. But most flowers grow in spring and summer.

25

The gardener carefully collects the seeds from

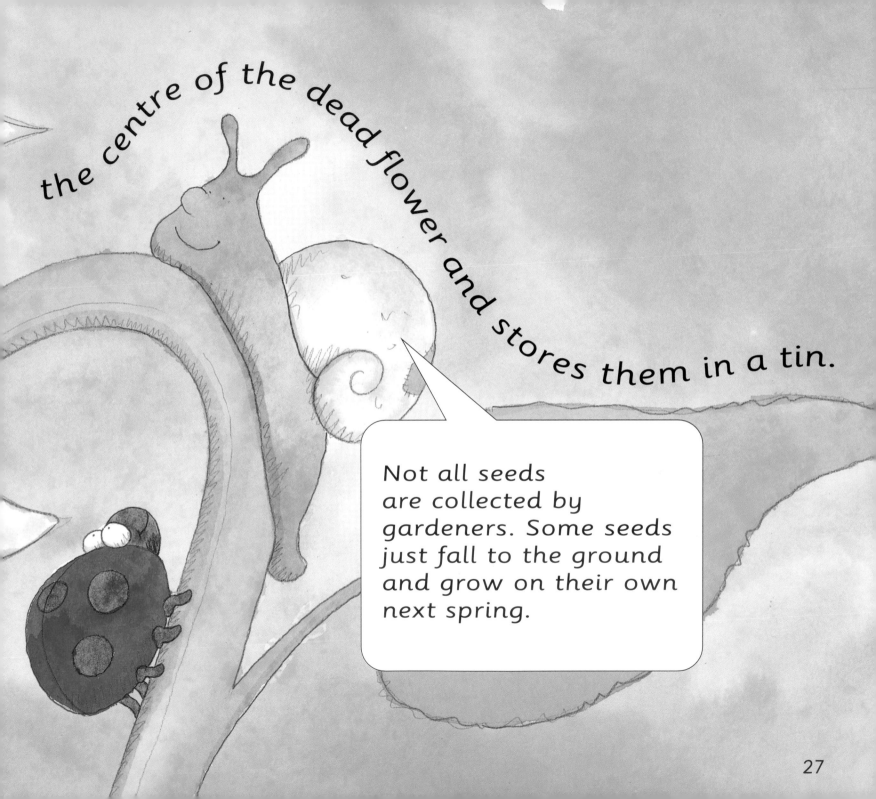

the centre of the dead flower and stores them in a tin.

Not all seeds are collected by gardeners. Some seeds just fall to the ground and grow on their own next spring.

Next spring he will sow them in the soil again.

Useful Words

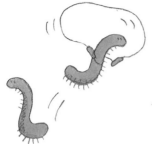

Bud
A flower that hasn't opened yet.

Nectar
A sweet juice inside a flower that attracts bees and butterflies.

Pollen
Yellow dust that helps plants make new seeds.

Root
The underground part of a plant that sucks food and water from the soil. Roots also help keep a plant in place.

Seed
The small hard part of a plant from which a new plant grows.

Seedling
A very young plant.

Shoot
The white stem growing out of a seed that becomes a plant.

The Sunflower

Pollen is the yellow dust found in the middle of a flower.

Insects carry pollen dust from one flower to another on their legs and wings.

Petals are the colourful parts around the middle of the flower.

Leaves capture energy from the sunlight and use it to make food for the plant.

A strong stem supports the plant.